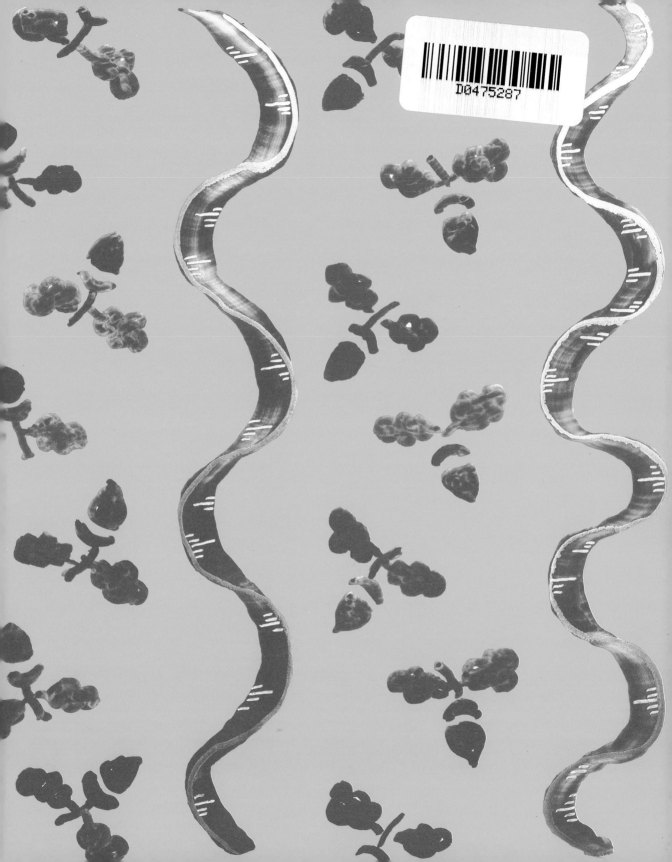

# To Have & To Hold

**box** (boks) *n*, sb.2 (Late OE. *box*, prob. -*\*bux*-, for late L. *buxid-*, *stem of buxis*, var. of L. *pyxis*, prop. box of box-wood. Cf. PYX Boist.]

**I. 1.** A case or receptacle usually having a lid.

The Shorter Oxford English Dictionary on Historical Principles
Third edition, 1973

# To Have
# & To Hold

## Decorative American Boxes

**Pat Ross**

*Text with Leisa Crane*

## Photographs by Keith Scott Morton

*Styling by Patricia O'Shaughnessy*

VIKING
STUDIO
BOOKS

VIKING STUDIO BOOKS
Published by the Penguin Group
Viking Penguin, a division of Penguin Books USA Inc.,
375 Hudson Street, New York, New York 10014, U.S.A.
Penguin Books Ltd., 27 Wrights Lane, London W8 5TZ, England
Penguin Books Australia Ltd., Ringwood, Victoria, Australia
Penguin Books Canada Ltd, 2801 John Street, Markham, Ontario, Canada L3R 1B4
Penguin Books (N.Z.) Ltd., 182–190 Wairau Road, Auckland 10, New Zealand

Penguin Books Ltd., Registered Offices:
Harmondsworth, Middlesex, England

First published in 1991 by Viking Penguin, a division of Penguin Books USA Inc.

1 3 5 7 9 10 8 6 4 2

Library of Congress Cataloging in Publication Data

Ross, Pat.
To Have and To Hold: the Sweet Nellie Book of decorative American boxes/
Pat Ross with Leisa Crane; photographs by Keith Scott Morton; styling by
Patricia O'Shaughnessy.

p. cm.
1. Boxes, Ornamental—United States—Themes, motives. I. Crane, Leisa.
II. Title.
NK3665.R67 1991
745.593—dc20 89-40798
ISBN 0-670-83061-5

Printed in Singapore
Set in Cochin
Designed by Frierson + Mee Associates, Inc.

# *Also by Pat Ross*

*With Thanks & Appreciation*

*The Pleasure of Your Company*

*With Love & Affection*

*Motherly Devotion*

*I Thee Wed*

*Formal Country*

### *For Children*

*Young and Female:*
*Turning Points in the Lives of*
*Eight American Women*

*What Ever Happened to the Baxter Place?*

*Molly and the Slow Teeth*

The *Meet M and M* Beginning Reader Books

*Hannah's Fancy Notions*

# *Acknowledgments*

Without the cooperative and creative input of many willing people, the success of networking, and just plain hard work, books such as this one would never move forward from the idea stage. I would like to credit and thank the many who brought *To Have & To Hold* from birth to book.

Sincere gratitude to all those dealers and collectors who helped us find the boxes for this book and who loaned us theirs: Cynthia Beneduce, Tom Dolan, Mimi McMennamin, Peter Emacura, Evan Hughes, Kate and Joel Kopp, David Drummond, Haje O'Neill, Jim Udell, Bill Strauss, George Korn, Richard Kemble, Jolie Kelter and Michael Malcé, Ruth Carey, Virginia Doherty, Pat and Connie Kent, David Schorsch, Judy and Jim Milne, Laura Fisher, Lynn Lorwin, Carol Wright, Kathleen Kohl, Diane Glenn, Ingrid Savage, Marilyn Breckner, and Susan Parrish. Helaine and Burton Fendelman, Gail Lettick, and

Linda Cheverton graciously allowed us access not only to their box collections but also to their homes for our photography. Victoria Dinardo thoughtfully closed her millinery shop so that we might photograph her box collection and her wonderful hats.

A number of museums, galleries, and libraries were generous with both their scholarship and their box collections. We benefited from their expertise during our research. Our appreciation goes to the Boscobel Historical Restoration—especially to Frederick Stanger, the director, Karen Dunn, and Pat Allen—for allowing our film crew into the wonderful mansion and onto the grounds, making this book richer for those shots. Appreciation also to Frank Miele and Bruce Bergmann at Hirschl & Adler Folk for trusting us not only with their box collection but also with the exemplary folk art pieces that enrich the photographs taken there. We were also supported in this project by The Museum of the City of New York, The Abby Aldrich Rockefeller Folk Art Center—especially Audrey Ritter there—The Shelburne Museum, and The Museum of American Folk Art, whose director of museum shops, Marie DiManno, was, as always, a real friend. Thanks also to the Whitney Museum's Store Next Door, The New York Society Library, The Cooper-Hewitt Library, Dennis Marnon of the Houghton Library, Harvard University, and Veronica McNiff of The Cooper-Hewitt Museum.

Friends and colleagues came to our rescue when we needed special pieces, props, and accessories: Nancy and Aileen Lubin; Gregory Castro and his shell collection; Ursus Books of New York for the antique maps on page 83; Pam and Kevin White; Lexington Gardens; Cris Anne's, for the dried-flower arrangement on page 32; our neighbors at Janet Russo, who loaned us the vintage jewelery on page 2; Ellen O'Neil; and Ivy Weitzman.

So many friends and family members made this their project too: Judy Crawford and Pat Lovejoy, who allowed us free run of their lovely homes for photography; Leonard Todd; Kate Williams; Allison Percival; and Ann Leonard Hardy, who knew all along that Keith and I would do a book together! Special thanks to Lois Perschetz, who helped me find a title when *To Have & To Hold* was just a wonderful new idea. The old family photographs and letters that decorate several pages of this book were dusted off and donated by my mother, Anita Kienzle, whom I put to work on every book!

The nitty-gritty work for this book began several years ago. Much appreciation to Cathy Struve, a student back then at The Brearley School, who applied herself to the task of gathering facts for the proposal. Then Leisa Crane brought her well-polished skills to the book with her usual dedication. On the set, Keith Morton's assistants, Ann Callahan and Debra DeBoise, helped make our long days rewarding

and fun. Patti O'Shaughnessy brought her unique
way of seeing artistic arrangements to each and every
shot. Behind the scenes, Beth Tudor and Eve Cantor
kept Sweet Nellie hopping.

Barbara Williams, my editor at Viking Studio
Books, had faith in this book from the outset, and I
would be lost without her vision and the beautiful
books she gives her authors. Viking Studio Books'
Publisher, Michael Fragnito, always has my affection
and respect for the way he deals with the ebbs and the
flows. At Writers House, Amy Berkower, my agent,
and her team—Sheila Callahan and Mabel Cramm—
save my life regularly, and deserve appreciation.

I know that I would have to travel far and wide
to find a photographer as good and as good-natured as
Keith Morton. Thank you, Keith, for including the
considerations of all of us in shots that can only be
described as the very best.

# Introduction

As a child, I often visited a favorite aunt who wore crisp white gloves, well-cut tweed suits, and a new hat for every occasion. Atop her closet shelves were the hatboxes that held what appeared to me at that impressionable age to be a vast number of exquisite creations. I often made lame excuses to visit her closet, and soon my interest became obvious and a bit of a family joke. Eventually, I was invited to freely explore her carefully stacked boxes, which were set on the closet floor just for me.

I loved the sturdiness of those cardboard forms, the elegance of the silk and grosgrain ties. A few boxes were covered in decorative papers; most were a distinguished gray or black, sometimes striped or patterned. During the photographing of this book, I experienced a touching sense of *déjà vu* when, at one location, I recognized three of the same orange-and-black hatboxes as my aunt had (page 11), with labels from a department store in Baltimore, where my aunt lived. Our emotional connection to objects from the past is undeniable, and is one reason we surround— even comfort—ourselves with such tangible incarnations of our memories.

By the time I was wearing hats to church in the fifties, they came in clear plastic boxes, staring out at the world rather vulgarly. It wasn't until many years later that pretty hatboxes would find favor once again, and that I would renew my love for decorative American boxes of all kinds.

On a vacation in Vermont some years ago, I visited The Shelburne Museum, a remarkable landmark that at that time was a rather well kept secret, emerging from years of renovation and expansion. I was thrilled and astounded by their extraordinary collection of boxes. A visit to museums such as the Shelburne, the Abby Aldrich Rockefeller Collection, and the Boscobel Restoration can open your eyes to the fascinating and rich array of American boxes that exists to be discovered and enjoyed.

Because boxes in museums and galleries are often given a pedestal presentation, we think of them as rare art objects. Remembering that all boxes were made to be used and to fill a specific function quickly brings us back to their humble origins, and to the social customs of a more civilized era. Historical societies and house tours provide less formal settings for the appreciation of how boxes were used and displayed in their time. Then, compartmentalization was an art as well as a necessity. There was a place for everything, and boxes provided that place.

The boxes in this book have been taken off their pedestals, so to speak, and photographed in home settings, showing how we may surround ourselves with boxes and make them a part of our rooms and our lives. Although many antique boxes require special care and handling, they existed in the past to be used and admired, and often continue in that tradition today. The boxes in *To Have & To Hold* represent only a sampling of the rich range of American boxes still readily available to anyone with the interest and the inclination to collect.

American boxes are the children of their British forebears, which were used in every conceivable way—from the ubiquitous tea caddy to tiny boxes for skin patches used as beauty marks. Inventive American settlers, longing for memories of their homeland, took advantage of the materials at hand and created boxes that brag of their spirited invention, bold creativity, and the personal details that no blueprint can provide. Many high-style American boxes were influenced by the styles of the furniture and fashion of the day. Other boxes were made by humbler folks, whose unskilled hands were more influenced by pure need and the guiding spirit of the heart. American boxes offer dignified formality, exceptional beauty, whimiscal charm, folksy character, quirky expression,

and sculptural appeal—sometimes all in the same box. Many of the boxes included may not be candidates for museum collections, yet they are treasured companions with historical meaning.

There's a certain kinship established by the possession of antique boxes. Clues, memories, and the indelible stamp of previous ownership linger in engraved initials or a thoughtful inscription, a lock of hair, a letter left behind, or the vague aroma of spices, tobacco, or pressed roses. Because boxes were handled, often daily, the touch of hand softens and personalizes them, leaving certain messages behind.

The interiors of boxes make our detective work even more intriguing. An undeniable mystery surrounds a closed box. The secret cache just beneath the lid is contained in a small private space, known only to its owner. When the lid is removed, it may reveal just a plain and disappointing deepness, or it may surprise us with imaginative artistry or a riot of color.

The tradition of box making continues today. American artisans with a healthy respect for the boxes of the past are re-creating antique boxes they admire, using the same painstaking skills and materials employed so long ago. Still other artisans are creating new boxes of their own invention. To bring *To Have & To Hold* up to date, we have included many of these newly made boxes.

Over the years, I have found special places and uses for all sorts of boxes, plain and fancy. My mother's father always remembered to save his cigar boxes for me when I was small, which I'd découpage to death! Years later, these boxes would still carry the mellow aroma of my grandfather's cigars and remind me of him.

My father's father made fine decorative boxes and chests as part of his custom furniture business in Germany. I own a small, baroquely carved mahogany chest, adorned with flowers, which he made, and my sister owns an extraordinary rosewood box, inlaid with an elegant flower and leaf design, which was made by our father when he apprenticed in our grandfather's workshop at the age of fifteen. So boxes are for me a third-generation interest. They fill my home and my shop, Sweet Nellie.

It's obvious that the popularity of decorative boxes is rising. Decorating magazines and catalogs show us boxes to accessorize every room. Antiques journals and auction publications let us know that antique boxes are eminently collectible, fun, and affordable. An increase in scholarship on the subject means that boxes old and new will continue to attract attention.

I hope that the many treasures in this book and the stories behind those treasures will make box owners, makers, or collecting enthusiasts out of all of you!

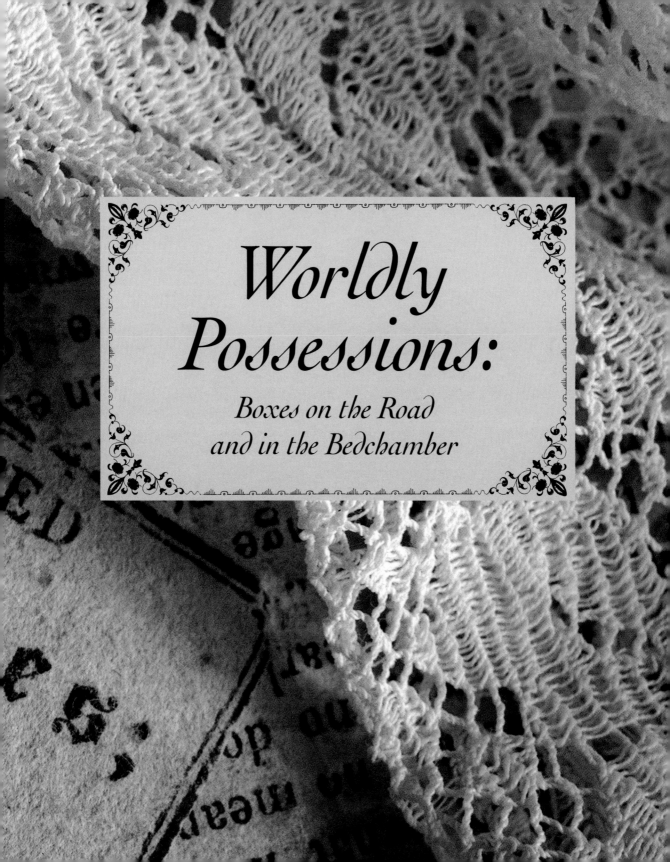

# Worldly Possessions:

## Boxes on the Road and in the Bedchamber

Aglimpse back in time enables us to appreciate the gracious accoutrements associated with travel in generations past. The portable boxes that were carried from the bedchamber onto a coach or a carriage—stacked high and lashed tightly on top— filled passersby with a sense of adventure and discovery as they imagined the finery carefully packed within. These boxes served as home away from home, containing the worldly possessions of the traveler: bandboxes covered with richly colored wallpapers; small chests made of weather-beaten hide and studded with brass; and colorful painted traveling boxes locked for safekeeping. Today, these antique boxes often show obvious signs of wear, but they are avidly sought by those who appreciate the reflections of the past in today's contemporary settings.

The rugged appeal of some travel boxes points to their appropriateness to early forms of transportation. Stagecoach travel was arduous, and the conditions that

**Signed by the Maker**
*Hannah Davis, known to her friends and neighbors as "Aunt Hannah," devised a way to make boxes from spruce and pine logs. She bartered with her neighbors for the newspaper that lined the boxes and for the colorful range of wallpapers covering them. Originally sold for twelve to fifty cents, today they command high sums. This particular box, from the collection of Pantry & Hearth, is beginning to show the signs of age and must be kept away from admiring hands and bright light.*

both travelers and belongings underwent called for hearty wooden or pressed-tin traveling companions, as well as leather and sealskin trunks designed to endure a berth on top of a coach. The more delicate band- and hatboxes, along with carpetbags, were carried inside on the owner's lap or under the seat.

The bandbox had its antecedent in Europe, where boxes were used to transport clothing and accessories, specifically men's neckbands. Nineteenth-century bandboxes were lightweight, made of paste-board or ash and pine. Their elegance of form and decoration made them cherished possessions. While many bandboxes were made commercially by box and wallpaper manufacturers, and were often sold to accompany merchandise, many other boxes were crafted by artisans who found a thriving cottage industry in bandbox production.

Miss Hannah Davis of Jaffrey, New Hampshire, now a legend among box collectors, created sturdy wooden boxes out of spruce logs. She covered her boxes with pieces of wallpaper that she obtained through bartering with her neighbors. At first, Miss Davis sold or bartered her goods locally. Later, she discovered a willing market in the eager young women who worked in the New England textile mills of the 1840s. She barely kept up with the demand, driving a wagon loaded with bandboxes in the summer and using a sleigh in the winter. With a small income at their disposal, the factory girls were happy to find such

**Traveling Pretty**

*The sweeping view of the Hudson River from the grand west entrance of the elegant Federal-style house at the Boscobel Historical Restoration provides an elegant temporary resting place for a selection from the museum's colorful collection of nineteenth-century bandboxes. These boxes journeyed aboard dusty wagons, stagecoaches, and finally aboard newfangled steam-powered trains, their popularity spanning fifty years.*

**History through Wallcoverings**

*Close inspection of these boxes from the Boscobel collection reveals, alongside the hand-blocked floral and landscape-covered boxes, paper depicting significant historical places and events. Counterclockwise from the lower right, Castle Garden, a concert hall in lower Manhattan, as seen circa 1830–1840; the Deaf and Dumb Asylum was located in New York City at Forty-ninth Street and Fifth Avenue, circa 1831, and the Erie Canal, also called The Great Canal, was completed in 1825 to great fanfare.*

5

a pretty way to carry their few belongings on visits home. They'd pack up their bedraggled factory things in the box and deck themselves out in fancy clothes, which before the journey were kept fresh in the same cherished bandbox, often protected by a drawstring-type cotton bag. The expression "You look as though you just stepped out of a bandbox" is thought to have come from this association.

In days when travel was lengthy and difficult, and when inns along the way offered little privacy and few amenities, the comfort of one's own possessions was like the company of a good friend. When the journey was over, travelers attended to the care of many belongings at home by storing them in boxes, often the same boxes that had accompanied them on their travels.

In early homes, where public and private spaces commingled out of necessity, chests and boxes often provided the only storage space for personal and domestic items. Before the idea of a separate bedchamber or bedroom was realized, there was no such thing as a room for personal belongings. Chests and boxes provided a limited measure of private space. Later, as homes became larger, more specialized areas—the bedroom and the boudoir—evolved as private living spaces. The boudoir—part dressing room and part sitting room—was sometimes a room unto itself, calling for its own special variety of box storage.

**Small and Narrow**
*Built adjacent to a fire-place, shallow closets such as this one at Boscobel had pegs for nightclothes that would be warmed by the heat of the fire nearby. In the absence of closet space, boxes, such as these from the Boscobel collection, and small chests were essential storage containers for everything from men's starched collars to women's ball gowns.*

Bedroom and boudoir boxes were needed to protect small items on top of the bureau and dressing table; in drawers, boxes held love letters, small trinkets, gloves, jewels, and fragile wearing apparel. In the closet, hats and other delicate finery could rest securely in pretty band- and hatboxes. Beyond the utility of storage, these boxes added a touch of individuality to the most intimate home space, where company was often received. A closet door left ajar might reveal a stack of pretty bandboxes. A drawer left open might show intricately painted trinket boxes that hinted of hidden gems. The stylishness of any fine travel box might hint of exciting trips past and future.

In a way, we, the heirs of antique boxes, benefit from the hardships of our ancestors. Were it not for their lack of storage space, we might not be treated to the boundless variety of such wonderful small treasures discovered in stately mansions and the most modest cottage dwellings. Were it not for our ancestors' travel inconveniences, we would not have access to the many containers that they made for both strength and beauty. History has repaid us in full.

### A Fashionable Height

Protecting a valuable beaver hat would have been the very important function of this stately high-hat-shaped pasteboard box from the collection of Pantry & Hearth. The fashionable height for the crown of men's hats changed from year to year, so it is likely that this hat and box remained a steady pair. The stylized floral hand-blocked wallpaper was an elegant choice for the box's covering. High hats have been popular since the end of the seventeenth century; changing fashion trends have resulted in an interesting historical progression of high-hat styles and high-hat boxes.

**Showing Off**
*Hats by Victoria Dinardo
cut elegant profiles as
they sit atop vintage
display stands.*

**A Tribute to Time
and Place**
*A shopping spree in the
1920s and 1930s may well
have resulted in an armful
of department store
hatboxes filled with the
latest styles. This dra-
matic nest of boxes from
the collection of Cynthia
Beneduce Antiques, stand-
ing out against the black
lacquer of an elegant
settee, is graced with the
likeness of a historic
monument — the Wash-
ington Monument of
Baltimore, Maryland.
The bright orange-and-
black hatboxes are from
the Hutzler Brothers
Company, a department
store there.*

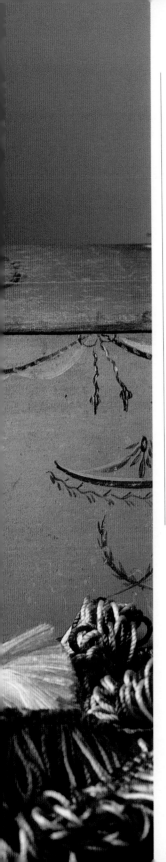

### A Classical Flourish

*The graceful swag design, an important part of the neoclassical-style decorating vocabulary, is an unusually elegant decoration for a box that is thought to have been a doll's blanket chest, complete with a secret drawer inside. Made of pine and decorated with a mustard-colored ground coat, fancy scrolling, and flourishes applied freehand, this miniature chest from the collection of E. G. H. Peter, Inc., is a copy of a full-size one. Although for child's play, it is fancy enough for showing off in any parlor or public room. It is from New England and dates from 1820 to 1830.*

### Dubious Protection

*This naughty puppy, who has made a plaything of his mistress's hat, provided some box maker with a humorous and endearing engraved image to use on a hatbox. Sewn together and unlined, the shape of the box bears an uncanny resemblance to a dog dish! Happily, the box, which I bought for my collection some years ago, contains its original contents, a ribbon-trimmed hat that now requires careful handling, as does the fragile paper box.*

## A Matter of Form
*The owner of Victoria Dinardo Fine Millinery collects wooden antique hat forms and uses them for display as well as for her design work. With every conceivable shape and style available to hat makers of the day, one can appreciate the demand for hatboxes of every size.*

## Inspired Chapeaux
*Victoria Dinardo designs enchanting hats in her shop in New York's SoHo district, where she displays them alongside her collection of vintage hatboxes and stylish black-and-white-striped hatboxes of her own design, likely collectibles for tomorrow.*

**A Shopping Spree**

*One can envision Ginger Rogers or Myrna Loy returning from a shopping spree exhausted, an array of hatboxes such as these, from the collection of Victoria Dinardo, dangling from both arms. Fashionable boxes of the day were, quite naturally, influenced by fashion styles and design trends.*

## Southwestern Style

*A very young collector, whose age can be calculated by the size of his cowboy boots on the left, was influenced by his parents' enthusiasm for antiques from the West and Southwest, especially for boxes to hold his cowboy memorabilia and paraphernalia. The Stetson hatbox is covered in a rich scene right out of the old West and came complete with its original hat, dating from the 1940s. Purchased at a flea market in Santa Fe by his mother, Haje O'Neill, it answered the young collector's perennial question, "What did you bring me?" The small Western trunk to the right is covered in hide and decorated with brass tacks. Here is one collector who seems to understand that it is never too early to begin!*

## Zeal Grown Cold

*Many people in the eighteenth and nineteenth centuries believed that religious fervor and piety alone would keep them warm, even in the winter chill of an unheated meetinghouse or carriage. Others believed that their foot stoves or warmers were sent from a merciful God via the peddling tinsmith. Useful wooden and tin boxes like the one from my collection, on the left, and from Pantry & Hearth, on the right, radiated warmth from the heated coals within. Dating from 1780 to 1860, all have handles for easy transport to the meetinghouse or carriage.*

## Traveling in Federal Style

*Handsome and durable, decorated travel boxes like these, from the collection of Hirschl & Adler Folk, brightened long journeys. These dome-topped pine boxes have been adorned with Federal-style swags, tassels, and sprays on a solid black ground. They are all attributed to the same maker, seemingly a professional who appears to have worked in central Massachusetts, and they may or may not have been a graduated set. The stenciled red and yellow patterns relate to designs used by ornamental painters at the time. All boxes are lined with a silver-tinged wallpaper that features a floral/vine pattern. They have their original hardware and date from 1825 to 1840. The plaid wool carriage blankets from Pennsylvania date from the mid-1900s.*

## Flying Colors

*The travel stickers beckoning one to exotic places were actually painted on this wooden suitcase in the 1920s, a humorous contrast to the simplicity of the box itself. This wooden box-turned-suitcase from the collection of Laura Fisher was perfectly adapted to the rigors of any kind of travel. Still intact, the mailing label shows it was sent by a soldier to his family home, the postmarks remaining as final evidence of the journey. This unusual suitcase sits alongside fine leather cases from the extensive suitcase collection of David Drummond.*

### Economy of Form

*A entire business can be contained in this bright wooden shoeshine box, one of my collectibles from the 1930s. The opening doubles as a handle as well as an area in which to store all the necessary shoe-shining supplies. A wonderful example of folk art from the more recent past, it still functions much as it did then, with the added bonus of being a conversation piece.*

### Bold Strokes

*A contemporary cork floor provides a harmonious background for this exuberant grain-painted storage box, which may have stored anything from family records to articles of clothing. The prominence of the lock suggests that the items stored within were of value to the owner, making travel with such a box plausible. This exceptional early piece from the collection of E. G. H. Peter, Inc., can be traced to Vermont or New Hampshire from about 1840.*

# Leisure Enjoyment:

## The Parlor

*C*omfortable and familiar, the front parlor in nineteenth-century homes was a safe haven, serving as an informal reception room and the place where close friends and kin gathered to share leisure time. As manners became less formal, activities such as indoor games, charades, conversation, reading, and music took place in this welcoming room. And for most of these activities, a box was a necessary component of the proceedings.

An eclectic and often eccentric collection of boxes served as safekeeping for everything from dominoes to marbles. A fancy candy box that at first held the fancy chocolates that it came with would later hold autumn leaves gathered by the children. Every so often, an old box can still be found that contains such odd and endearing tokens.

The Victorian front parlor contained a mad array of bric-a-brac, not the least of which was held in boxes. The Victorians' avid interest in nature might be

**Osborne's Finest**

*Unused and unspoiled, this box of Osborne's American Toy Water-Colours from the collection of Linda Cheverton dates from the mid-nineteenth century and contains all twelve colors of ready-to-use cake paints original to the box. Each cake is embossed with a delicate shell design. Mr. Osborne perfected the first American cake paints in this form during the early 1820s, making the outfitting of the paint boxes of many aspiring American artists of the time more agreeable, as a substantial British tax on imported paints had made them prohibitively expensive.*

represented in quirky boxes containing shells, eggs, feathers, leaves, flowers, and moss. The flowering of the domestic arts necessitated paint boxes, musical-instrument boxes, and sewing boxes, many decorated by the owner in the latest style of fashion.

Antique boxes do not always come complete with a history. It is part of the wonderful guessing game of owning an old box to pay close attention to the box's unique features and then use your wit and wisdom to make an educated guess as to its purpose and place in the home. It is likely that an elaborate penwork sewing box was meant for showing off when visitors came to call. It is a good guess that a grain-painted box containing a few family photos may have held the images of ancestors in some fine parlor. Handsome boxes that spoke well of the family's standing were often passed down from generation to generation and assigned new uses in the parlor.

Today's homes may contain a range of parlor boxes from the past—everything from silver tea caddies to primitive paint boxes—in ways both formal and casual that please us, assist us, and help us gather together our own loose ends.

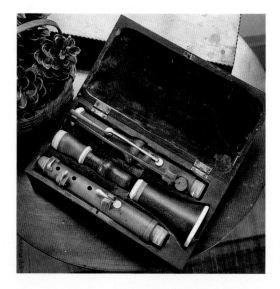

**Keeping Up Appearances**
*A musical-instrument box was created not only to hold a musician's priceless possession, in this case a finely wrought early wooden flute, but also to live up to a standard of excellence. Here, two flute boxes from the collection of the Boscobel Restoration feature delicate inlay work, a proud display case for any musician who considered such decoration a sign of accomplishment and social grace.*

## A Naturalist's Treasure Box

*One of my favorite posses-
sions is this ordinary
cigar box that was turned
into an unusual cache for
birds' eggs. Penciled in
longhand inside the lid is
a list of bird names and a
guide to the placement of
the corresponding eggs
within the box. The
owner, possibly a Victo-
rian nature enthusiast,
hand-built twenty small
compartments within the
cigar box and gently
cushioned each space with
cotton or lamb's wool.
Eggs stored in the box
include those of the great
crested flycatcher, the
thrush, the cowbird, and
the turtledove. The box
seems a natural accompa-
niment to the one-of-a-
kind painted birdhouse by
Daniel Hale on the right.*

## An Unassuming Collection

*It would be thoughtless to neglect the countless simple and unassuming utilitarian boxes—pasteboard and wooden alike—that provided storage for hundreds of items in times past, many of which remain in constant service today. Here, a pleasing variety shows how an old collection of tops has found a permanent home in a plain brown paper box, alongside boxes of assorted shapes and sizes holding everything from hairpins and pen nibs to sewing supplies and starched collars. Whether or not such old boxes will gain in value is a matter of opinion. The true value is in the eyes of the owner—in this case, Leisa Crane—whose fondness keeps cares about the dollars and cents of collecting at bay.*

## Neat as a Pin

*Pasteboard pin boxes such as this one, though humble and practical, held precious commodities in early households. Although the first all-in-one pins were invented by an American, Lemuel Wellman Wright, in 1824, they remained in short supply during much of the century. This pin box features a small round storage area and a tomato-shaped fabric pincushion, also called a pinpillow, on its lid. A pincushion would have been repaired and mended regularly with scraps from the workbag, kept for many years. This pleasing assortment of sewing accessories, all from the collection of Pantry & Hearth, includes a whimsical carrot pincushion and essential instruments for measuring.*

## Victorian Ornamentation

*The high Victorian period produced elaborate designs on decorative objects, in this case a romantic black painted box from the collection of Linda Cheverton that is well suited to the family parlor, where it could be admired by visitors who came to call. A miniature mother-of-pearl fan has been applied to the top of the box along with various other hand-painted images, creating a collage-type effect that invites close inspection.*

## Decoration Belies Function

*Disguised in a pretty sewing case such as this one from the Boscobel Restoration collection, a needle and thread would be fit to appear in any room of the house. This cone-shaped wooden case, sometimes called a nécessaire, pulls apart into three sections, the top section containing a spool for thread. Beautifully decorated with a painted rose and lily of the valley, the case is topped with a mushroom-shaped ivory finial. It may have been a souvenir from an overseas trip.*

### Quill Art

An interesting contrast to Native American Indian boxes decorated with dyed porcupine quills is this Anglo-Indian quill box thought to be from the British colony of Ceylon. This box, like many popular quill-decorated items from the mid-nineteenth century, made its way into American homes through merchants, traders, and sailors. The porcupine quills are set side by side into a wooden box. The ivory inlay is set into the rosewood edging. This quill box from the collection of David Drummond works well as part of an arrangement on an elaborately carved mahogany table.

### Classical Elegance

The engraved borders and swags on this elegant early-nineteenth-century ivory box from the collection of the Boscobel Restoration give it a classic formality that is well suited to its high-style surroundings and sympathetic to the design on the two porcelain vases. Lined with pearwood, the small box may have been used for snuff. The presence of a lock might indicate that the contents were as valued as the box itself in its day.

**Genteel Avocations**

*This elegant Regency sewing box dating from about 1810, from the collection of the Boscobel Restoration, was naturally suited to the parlor, where plain sewing was shunned in favor of fancy needlework, at least while company was at hand. Rectangular in shape, with an unusual domed top that opens in the center for easy access to needlework and the necessary sewing accessories, the wooden box is decorated with penwork—sometimes called "poor man's chinoiserie"—showing animals and allegorical figures. Although this example is probably English, American women in fine homes would have sought such elegance from American or English sources.*

**Diminutive Collectibles**

*The one attribute that these delightful small boxes have in common is their size. Attracted to boxes that fit easily into the palm of one's hand, the owner of this collection, Ingrid Savage of Hat & the Heart, was drawn to them for their small-scale charm. The oval 1800s snuff box is made of horn and is English. To its right, a perfect size for thimbles and tiny sewing notions, is an embossed brass egg from the American Victorian period. The delicate chain might have looped through a finger or a belt. Above it, the black lacquer papier-mâché box with mother-of-pearl inlay work is also Victorian. Hand-constructed with gold-foil cutwork edging, the remaining box contains a carefully cut out and applied image of a cozy-looking cabin that completes the arrangement.*

**Charming Interiors**

*The finishing interior touches of this early grain-painted chest from New Hampshire, from the collection of Dr. and Mrs. Jay Kuhlman, provide a pleasant surprise. Lined with softly colored hand-blocked wallpaper, the box is inviting when left open, displaying old family photographs and letters. Dating from the 1850s, the box has a unique keyhole, which contains the original key and is decorated in a different grain-painting technique from the rest of the box, a pattern that is then repeated at the bottom corners.*

**Sunburst**

*A simple yet graphically bold approach to the inlay technique, which uses different colors of woods, adorns the lid of a wooden box from the collection of Laura Fisher, which may have held trinkets or jewels for either a man or a woman. Its square shape and easily portable size allow us a variety of guesses as to its use, which is one of the wonderful mysteries of any box's history.*

## Love to Mother

*Complete with a matching presentation card inscribed "Love to Mother," this elegant candy box (from the Artstyle Chocolate Company, circa 1930), owned by Sandra Washburn, was as much a gift as were the confections it contained. Coming from a time when giving candy was considered a part of proper etiquette, the delicate open-fan design on the silken fabric surface must have delighted the mother who received it. No doubt yesterday's recipient would be amazed to learn of the gift box's value as a collectible today.*

## Once Humble

*Thrifty women were grateful for even the smallest scraps of wallpaper, which they cleverly used to adorn pretty boxes that would be used for trinkets, cherished silk ribbon, odd buttons, artificial flowers, and pieces of coveted lace. The delicate wallpaper box from my collection, pictured here on the left, is a collector's dream, as it gives several clues to its provenance. Made from an old cigar box stamped "PA." on the bottom, it is lined with a Lancaster, Pennsylvania, newspaper, The New Era, dated "Saturday 7, 1880." This charming made-over cigar box has held up well over the years, increasing its value today. The miscellaneous small trinket boxes on the right, also from my collection, are replicas made with old wallpaper, which is still saved by thrifty box makers.*

2. What do y...

tion

...1 Such facto...

...set one under anoth...

2 The cyphes placed at

the factor  are to be

then the same numb...

*Exam*

Pints

476000

176

33320000

176

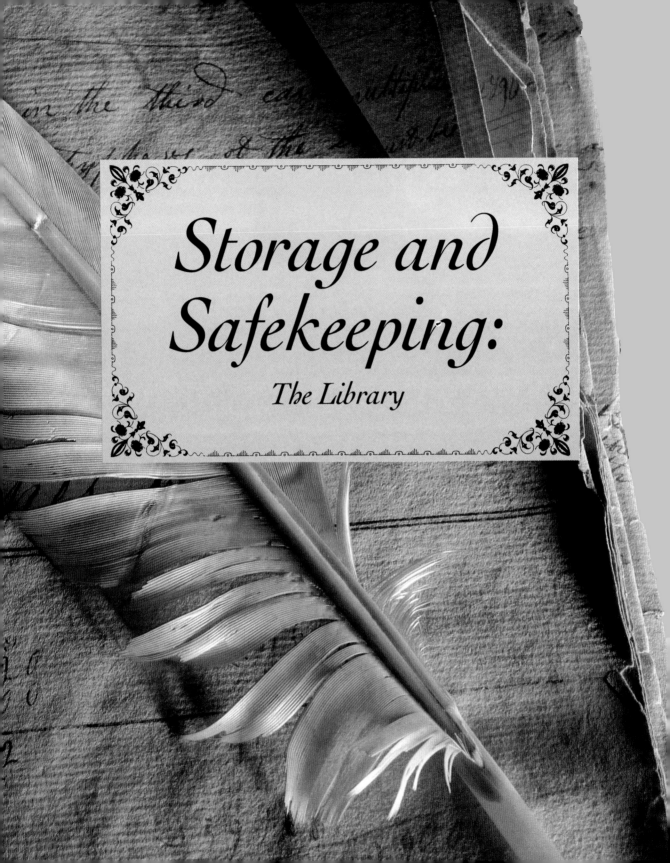

# Storage and Safekeeping:

## The Library

A magnificent grain-painted document box complete with its original brass hardware once held a family's complete financial records. Today it decorates a hall table, where guests and acquaintances admire it as they pass. In a home office, a humble tin box, festively painted, dating from the turn of the century, holds a student's research cards. Once confined to the library or study, these boxes now find their place in nearly every room of today's home, united by their connection to yesterday.

From land deeds and other official documents to elaborately penned love letters and personal diaries, many forms of written and printed communication required storage and safekeeping, and subsequently gave birth to some of our handsomest and most collectible historical boxes. Closets, compartmentalized desks, and grand case furniture, as we know them today, have not always existed. The need to protect valuable documents and keep family business in order has. This

**Taken to Fancy**

*Surely one of a kind, this gaily polka-dotted document or storage box was created when the artist's fancy prevailed. The large primitive latch lock looks out of proportion to the thin wire pull on the domed lid. The outer edges of the box are striped in a cheerful yellow paint, completing the decoration of this simple wood construction. A delightful antique painted chair is a compatible resting place for this whimsical box from the collection of Linda Cheverton.*

made necessary a variety of utility boxes—such as desk, deed, book, document, and money boxes, employed for those specific purposes.

Perhaps because there was a strong sense of importance and worth connected to the contents of these boxes, early box owners took special pride in the way their boxes were decorated and ornamented. The simplest kitchen box might hold candles, but a more prestigious presentation was *de rigueur* for the box containing family marriage and birth records.

By its very nature, a utility box would have done its job satisfactorily if it had merely protected what was stored in its confines; however, in late-eighteenth- and early-nineteenth-century homes, it was called upon to be an ornament as well. A colorful and pleasing box kept out in the open could bring life to a drab room and was a source of pride to its owners. Flat broad sides and dome-lidded tops made boxes especially well suited to a variety of decorative techniques.

Painted decoration was at its peak form during the first fifty years of the nineteenth century. Decoration was done by everyone from ornamental painters to itinerant artists to amateurs at home. The vivid decoration that dominated this period came in many forms, including plain all-over surface painting, grain painting, stenciling, striping and banding, and freehand ornamentation. Boxes became small canvases for artists, who would adorn them with imitative or wildly fancy graining, ornamentation such as scrolls and

**Lightening the Task at Hand**
*One can imagine that this pine box, from the collection of Hirschl & Adler Folk, brightened the interior of its owner's home. Probably used to store important papers, it wears a fanciful coat of red paint with putty-applied decoration. The brass rosette and pull are probably original. It was made in Rhode Island around 1830.*

## Geometric Ornamentation

*Three handsome document boxes displaying geometric artistry, from the collection of Hirschl & Adler Folk, serve as useful a purpose today as they did when they were created. The solid ground coat of paint and geometric striping were a popular form of ornamentation in New England during the period from 1830 to 1835. The largest box has eight compartments, each two inches high, at the bottom of the box, separated by pine dividers. All three boxes once had locks, and all have hinged lids. Important documents such as land deeds and marriage and birth records might have been locked safely within.*

tassels, and even verdant landscapes. Wooden marquetry and inlay boxes offered endless possibilities for dazzling design. For boxes made of tin, painted decoration served to both embellish and protect the tin from rust.

Boxes found in country homes often mimicked their more expensive city counterparts. Fine boxes were made of wood whose grain and luster could stand on their own; painted ornamentation was applied to highlight the natural beauty of the wood. Country boxes required imagination — and often deception — to attain their glory.

By the beginning of the nineteenth century, greater prosperity allowed for both more material goods in each household and more boxes to contain them. Various desk boxes, such as stamp, string, and pen boxes, gradually made their way onto the American desk.

To keep possessions out of harm's way, many boxes were fitted with a lock and key, and many had handles to facilitate their use during travel. Very often the ornamental hardware stands out and adds significant value. The presence today of the original key is cause for celebration.

**Locked Away
for Keeps**
*Over the years, many document boxes had their locks, keys, and decorative hardware lost or replaced. This small grain-painted document box from the collection of Helaine and Burton Fendelman has the original hinged lid, sturdy brass handle, and fancy working lock. The painted finish was achieved by vinegar painting, a popular technique of the nineteenth century. Small boxes with locks such as this one were often used for travel. At home, they stored envelopes and folded documents, being easily accessible from a desk or shelf.*

**Early Abstraction**
*A repetitive design in two colors gives this exceptional document box from the collection of Helaine and Burton Fendelman an abstract appeal that is as at home in the modern world as it was during the early part of the nineteenth century. A grain-painted ground over pine is enhanced by a repeated all-over comb-painted pattern in vibrant colors. Despite the amount of decoration on the box, which is probably from New England, the patterns and colors balance perfectly.*

Today's home library or study generally contains a capacious desk, shelves for books and whatnots, and cabinets for storing our jumbles of paper. Yet no matter how generous the desk drawers or how expansive the shelving, there is still the need for boxes to contain and organize the overflow. Attractive historical boxes continue to serve their original purposes while giving us satisfaction through visual beauty and a connection to the past.

**Personalized**

*Yesterday's boxes provide perfect catchalls for today's desk clutter, even if they were not originally intended for use at a desk. This plum pantry box, which retains much of its original paint, was made in New England around 1840. The formal style of the lettering of the initials "F.M." contrasts pleasingly with the simplicity of the box. Estate records show that the box belonged to one Florene Maine. It is now a part of the box collection at Hirschl & Adler Folk .*

**Stencil Excellence**

*Here are two fine examples of stenciled document boxes, from the collection of Hirschl & Adler Folk, that may be admired for their excellence and rarity. The box on the left is from upstate New York, circa 1830. The delicate scallop border and other predominant stencils are white gold. Made by Ransom Cook between 1820 and 1830, the fancy document box on the right features grain-painted decoration as well as finely shaded stenciling. The stencils are framed by a border of stylized grain painting.*

## An Individual Approach

*While most of the stencils on this dome-top box have been applied in a single color—silver or red—the free-spirited set of four red circles painted near the handle has received a hand-drawn addition of crossed, wavy yellow lines. Both the choice and the placement of the stencils give this box from the collection of Hirschl & Adler Folk a more individualistic and less polished look than many of the stylized stenciled boxes that survive from the same period. This box is from New England, possibly Massachusetts, circa 1825 to 1830.*

### Elegant Yet Earthy

*Storage containers were kept in public areas of the home, and so they were often festively decorated to brighten their settings. Certainly the pleasingly timeworn red-orange ground color on this box, from the collection of Linda Cheverton, allows the somewhat abstract stencil decoration—a daisy, a chrysanthemum, or a fireworks display—to stand out. This piece, from the 1850s, is made of tin. Tinplate was produced in the United States starting in 1829, making tinwork boxes readily available here. Previously, tin sheets had to be imported.*

### Optical Illusions

*Marquetry, or the technique of applying designs onto wood veneers, found great favor in this country during the late nineteenth and early twentieth centuries. For a woodworker, the surfaces of a box resembled a miniature stage on which many elaborate productions could be mounted. Exotic influences may be seen in the complex geometric patterns on this nineteenth-century marquetry box from the collection of Laura Fisher, which boasts a raised center panel, mitered corners, and bun feet. Many different woods have been selected and arranged in a design that celebrates optical originality.*

**Saturday Evening Girls**

*Some of the most exceptional pottery of the early twentieth century was made during the Arts and Crafts movement, and much of it was made and decorated by women. This pottery grouping from the collection of Helaine and Burton Fendelman, which includes two desk boxes, was produced in Boston by an association of young immigrants who met on Saturday evenings for reading and craft activities, which eventually included ceramics. The association called itself The Saturday Evening Girls. Their pottery was sometimes referred to as SEG pottery. Paul Revere Pottery was an outgrowth of the SEG. Each highly glazed and incised piece in this collection is initialed and dated on the bottom — "12/17 A.M.," meaning it was made in December 1917 by someone with the initials A.M.*

**Celebrating the Red, White, and Blue**

*Throughout our history, patriotic themes have dignified and embellished decorative objects. The document box pictured here, from the collection of James and Bonnie Udell, is an example of this. An arrowlike line of woods has been inlaid to form a stylish border, and a central banner with four flags has been inlaid into the top of the box. The colors are still bright after more than a century of use, and the box is in mint condition. One assumes that such a distinguished box would have been used for documents of quite some worth, perhaps by a politician. The 1860 flag and outstanding 1870 American oil painting, which appear courtesy of Susan Parrish Antiques, make a perfect backdrop.*

# Hearth and Home:

## The Kitchen

The grand-scale fireplace with its welcoming hearth was a familiar gathering place for early American settlers. They shared the warmth and light of this common space out of simple necessity. There they did their reading and record-keeping, observed their daily devotions, and welcomed strangers into their company. It was in this same room that our forebears prepared and ate their meals.

By the end of the eighteenth century, a prosperous home would have had not only a kitchen but additional rooms for sugaring, preserving, and storing food. There was a pantry, a butt'ry, a milkroom, a shed, a shed chamber, and an attic. And in each room and for each function, boxes played a vital role as storage containers.

Large stores of grain and other food staples were bought in quantity and stored in barrels or large boxes. For daily use, smaller amounts of these staples were transferred to other boxes kept in the pantry or

**To Market, to Market**
*A glimpse back into the nineteenth-century country store and pantry is offered by these mint-condition food tins from the collection of Pantry & Hearth. Tin containers were a good means for strong, airtight convey-ance and storage of perishables. Also, producers welcomed the advertising potential that the surfaces afforded. Early metal boxes were decorated with paper labels, stenciling, or paint. Since paper labels were easily damaged in handling and storage, they are especially valued today. The deep bin here was a coffee bin, meant to sit on the floor of the general store.*

kitchen. Coarse salt, for instance, would have been stored in large quantities in barrels; smaller amounts would be kept conveniently in the kitchen, in lidded salt boxes; and at the table, salt cellars held salt for immediate use.

Sugar, spices, and herbs were all stored in quantity. Smaller amounts of these staples were kept in wooden pantry boxes, many of which could be purchased in nests of graduated sizes. Pantry boxes could be purchased from the cooper if the man of the house did not have the time or the talent to make them.

The nests of oval storage boxes with carefully fitted lids that were made and sold by the Shaker community represent the epitome of pantry-box construction and design. The Shaker philosophy that "beauty rests on utility" governed their exquisite craftsmanship and pure design. As many as eighteen processes were performed by hand for each box. These oval—also called "nice"—boxes were sold to the outside world, along with grain measures, firkins, sewing boxes, and carriers. Many Shaker boxes, however, were kept for the Shaker community itself. Today, Shaker boxes are among the most valued and sought-out collectibles.

A well-lit fire and candlelight were as important to family life as the food supply. It is no wonder, then, that the tinderbox and the candle box were vital kitchen furnishings. The circular tinderbox was made

**Spice with Design in Mind**
*Some design-minded owner may have been the one who festively embellished this metal spice set with stars and banners. Most often, however, tin spice boxes were simply painted black and put to use holding freshly clipped spices from the garden to be ground later with a mortar and pestle. But here, an artistic spirit prevailed, and happily so for today's collectors. This spice set from my collection is thought to be from the early part of this century. The painted decoration seems to have been a later addition.*

## Remembrance of Kitchens Past

*Two wooden spice box
sets, late-nineteenth-
century factory pieces,
retain their homey charm.
The large round boxes,
labeled "Spices" in
stenciled lettering,
generally held seven to
eight small canisters, each
labeled with the individual
spice names, ranging from
Cinnamon to Pepper. The
set on the left atop the
nineteenth-century spice
shelf, from the collection
of Judith and James
Milne, is made of birch
veneer with tin bindings;
the set below, from the
collection of Pantry &
Hearth, is made entirely
of wood. The spice tower,
also from the collection of
Pantry & Hearth,
resembles those of English
origin. Often, the
lingering scents of spices
from many years ago
permeate the wood,
providing an additional
treat on close inspection.*

out of metal to safeguard the flammable materials within. Candles were a luxury in colonial days, and were burned to the very end of the wick. That the candle supply was carefully safeguarded is not surprising, and special boxes were designed to hold the candles after the autumn candle making was completed.

We seem to have come full circle to the large family kitchen as a place where community spirit and family activities are shared. That same tradition extends to the boxes we use, whether old, new, or reproduction. Yesterday's kitchen boxes bring a special hand-hewn charm to our sophisticated appliance-oriented world.

Many antique kitchen boxes continue to serve their intended purpose of storing food and utensils. Very often, however, they decorate and bring warmth and a sense of the past to our most used room.

**Bees in Boxes**

*This group of small wooden boxes from the Forager House Collection are bee boxes, structures with a fascinating history and growing appeal as collectibles. The bee boxes pictured here, with their various openings, sections, and sliding devices, are all handmade and offer a variety of inventive architectural styles. Many types of boxes were used for husbanding bees, including miniature hives, swarming boxes, finder's tracking boxes, queen nurseries, introducing cages, queen-rearing hives, and the observatory hive box, which was intended for use in the office or kitchen. Today's owner is generally happier with a beeless box in the kitchen!*

**Handle with Care**

*It was possible in the first decades of the twentieth century to send eggs by parcel post. This sturdy metal mailing box enabled a Willimantic, Connecticut, farmer to send four dozen eggs to a patron in New Haven, who then mailed the empty box back to him. The postage cost, revealed by the affixed stamps, was forty-two cents. Instructions printed on a card pasted inside the lid reveal that for five cents' insurance, the post office would pay for any broken eggs. Conversation pieces such as this unusual egg box (from my collection) are still reasonably priced at flea markets and tag sales, and they add a sense of history to any kitchen.*

**Folk Art**
**Past and Present**

*An old wooden egg basket from the collection of Ruth Carey holds an even dozen of Jane Pollack's exquisitely painted eggs, decorated using the ancient Ukrainian Easter-egg method of wax resist and dyes, more familiarly known as batik. Each egg is a masterpiece of American patchwork quilt design.*

### Stark and Striking

*Hanging wooden wall boxes like these from the collection of the Boscobel Restoration are among the most visually striking types of utilitarian kitchenware. The boxes shown here might have kept soap, pumice, and candles out of the reach of the elements. Before the advent of the first crude matches, tinderboxes, such as the one pictured here on the table, also from the collection of the Boscobel Restoration, were an essential item in every home. Containing flint, steel, and a piece of tinder—frequently old linen or cotton—they provided the essential means to light the fire that warmed a drafty room. The tin tinderbox shown has a place on its lid to set a candle—a ready carrier for the newly struck flame.*

### Borrowed Light

*Today, when the flip of a switch can fill a ballroom or a stadium with light, it is difficult to relate to the days when lighting was not a uniform comfort and making daily provision for light was essential. The simple palm-sized tin candleholder pictured, from the collection of Pantry & Hearth, is portable. When used for traveling, it would allow a small amount of personal light; in a home emergency, it would be useful as the carrier of a flame "borrowed" from a neighbor. Unable to produce its own spark, the box is divided into two sections, one to store the tiny candle and the other to hold matches or tinder. The beeswax candle sits in a hinged cup that folds conveniently into the box when not in use. The candleholder rests on a utilitarian wooden box with a sliding lid used to store household candles.*

### A Handsome Trio

*The appearance of even the most sophisticated kitchen would be enhanced by this collection of rustic wood firkins with original painted finishes. Firkins, also called sugar buckets, once served as storage containers. Shaker firkins were often used to store applesauce. These early examples from the collection of Laura Fisher — possibly Shaker — have wooden hoops with finger laps. Machine-made examples from later in the nineteenth century have nails securing the hoops, and recent factory-made firkins have wooden or iron hoops.*

### Peddling Their Wares

*Itinerant peddlers of the nineteenth century carried tinware packed in huge baskets as they traveled the countryside searching for kitchens in need of their wares. Later, they made their journeys on horseback and in their legendary painted carts, as the "tin man" became an indelible part of the American scene. Boxes made of tinplate, a sheet of iron rolled thin and coated on both sides with layers of molten tin, were often japanned, then stenciled or decorated freehand. The gaily decorated floral tinware pictured here, from the collection of Helaine and Burton Fendelman, includes a deed box, two canisters, and a wall box, a remarkably vivid collection of decorated pieces. Decorated tinware had regional characteristics that aid the collector in attributing it to an area or workshop.*

## An Apple for the Teacher

*A pair of wooden lunch boxes from the collection of Laura Fisher represent both handmade and commercially produced goods. The rectangular lunch box was handmade in the late nineteenth century, and has dovetailed edges and brass fittings. The other lunch box, a factory-produced item, bears the label "The 20th Century Ventilated Lunch-Box." The manufacturer of the new improved lunch box was so sure of the modern advantages of his design that he warned potential imitators of his intention to take out letters of patent, a warning that was given in detail on the inside of the detachable lid. Today's lunch-box collectors are a small but devoted group who covet such rare examples.*

## Boxed In

*A box seat in this Colosseum-like version of a nineteenth-century mousetrap might not be so bad, were it not for the obvious outcome for the mouse! Many inventors patented a variety of boxlike traps, such as the ones pictured here from the collection of Pantry & Hearth—metal, wood, or both—to deal with an age-old problem. In 1883, L. H. Mace & Co. offered three varieties of mousetrap: "common," "delusion," and the "wheel," which accommodated eight victims. For the collector seeking the extraordinary, the mousetrap's the thing.*

## Celebrating Sugar

*Sugar, an expensive delicacy in colonial America, was bought in large cones, or as pieces cut off a loaf from the grocer, and was powdered for table and baking and used sparingly. It seems fitting, then, that some pantry boxes would be decorated more elegantly to celebrate their valuable contents. Whether confined to the pantry or kept in a more visible and open space, this "Sugar" box from the collection of Helaine and Burton Fendelman must have delighted all who encountered it. Thought to be from Maine and of Shaker origin, the box has beautiful finger laps where joined, and dates from the first quarter of the nineteenth century.*

## A Contagious Pattern

*The lively dottings on this grain-painted storage box—as though the box or the box's owner were influenced by a bout of chicken pox—echo the roundness of the box itself with great success. The dotting design was done by applying solvent to the painted surface with the tip of a brush, causing the paint to run slightly outward from the center. A flat lid fits tightly on the box, which has vertical seams secured with nails. Thought to be from the first quarter of the nineteenth century, this box from the collection of Helaine and Burton Fendelman is a rare find. It is displayed perfectly on an appliqué "penny" table rug that, coincidentally, echoes the box's design.*

### The Appeal of Milk Paint

*Very little is known about this sturdy blue pantry box found at a Massachusetts flea market. The box, from my collection, was originally made with square nails , but has been repaired many times over the years with a variety of nails and crude staples. It is probable that the appealing blue milk paint was added at a later date, since it does not show the same signs of distress. Resembling a cheese box in shape and size, it may have been used to store hearty New England cheddar. Appreciated more for its appearance than for its storage value, this box should be seen and not used.*

### A Matter of Prestige

*American and English knife boxes from the collection of the Boscobel Restoration sit side by side on a beautiful mahogany sideboard, symbols of social importance in any early dining room, since owning silver was a matter of great prestige. The rare and elegant American knife box (right), one of a pair, is made of curly mahogany, edged with inlay, and features an inlaid star inside the slanting lid. The interior of the box is fitted with an inlaid frame that is grooved for the silver knives. To keep the family silver safe, the boxes were fitted with a molded brass lock, making this late-eighteenth-century pair all the more desirable.*

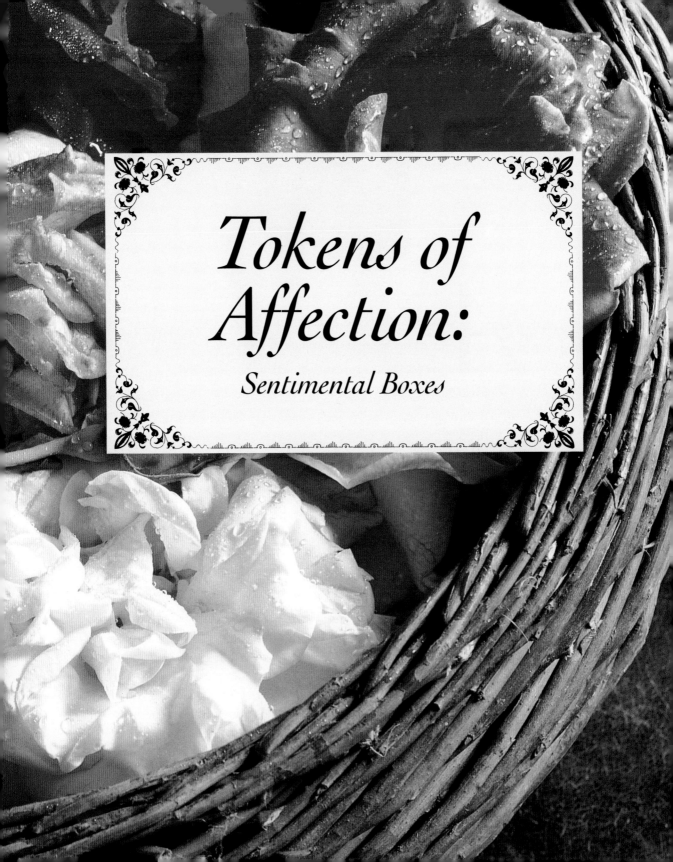

# Tokens of Affection:

## Sentimental Boxes

$A$ mateur hands working in unison with the heart have long celebrated the box form for the personal expression it offers. For a variety of reasons—creative urges, long hours to fill, an affectionate heart—many such boxes were created as gifts or presentation pieces. Although these boxes served practical purposes, their truly one-of-a-kind appearance distinguishes them as the most personally appealing of all boxes.

Both men and women created these tokens of affection. Many were created within the home. Taught by publications such as *Godey's Lady's Book, Peterson's Magazine,* and *Miss Leslie's Magazine* that there was "no excellence without industry," amateurs created boxes for giving as gifts, or donating to bazaars, as well as for purely personal uses. Even if fashioned by trends and guided by careful instructions, the results more often than not reflect the unique personality of the maker. Choice of material, shape, and personalized adornment

**Paper Treasures**
*This very special box belonged to an industrious young girl named Harriet, who apparently received numerous Rewards of Merit from her teachers and chose to embellish a box with them. Harriet pasted her many rewards and commendations artistically on a wooden box that was first covered with wallpaper and lined with newsprint. On the front, she placed a handmade sticker showing a leaping deer. Harriet's precious box, probably from the middle of the nineteenth century, is from the collection of Linda Cheverton.*

gives these homemade articles their charming individual hallmarks.

Many boxes were made without the benefit of instruction, however, and these inspired objects are especially sought after today for their individual charm. Tiny paper containers were turned into miniature treasure boxes to be given away or to be used to store tiny tokens—perhaps gifts from faraway friends. Fabric scraps, paper die-cuts, and a far-reaching imagination allowed someone rich in intent but poor in materials to create a small work of art.

Outside the home, boxes were often fashioned by sailors, whalers, prisoners, and itinerant artisans who had long hours to pass. Although some such boxes were inevitably sold or traded, many were created for a wife, sweetheart, mother, or friend far away. Materials at hand often included rope, cigar boxes, fruit crates, straw, shells, and whale ivory.

Tramp art—the whimsical and truly individualistic layered and notch-carved construction and decoration done throughout the United States from 1860 through 1920—is a relative newcomer to the popular collectibles scene, having been overlooked for too long. Mistakenly thought to have been done by tramps and hoboes, tramp art pieces were actually made by itinerant craftsmen and amateurs, who often found the inspiration for their patterns in magazines such as *Mechanics Illustrated*. Thin pieces of scrap wood, often from crates and cigar boxes, were built up and glued

### Small Treasures

*Here, two unique paint-and-collage boxes leave much for us to imagine about their history. The fact that they were both made in Rhode Island in the third quarter of the nineteenth century is known; however, the maker or makers are unknown. Constructed from existing paper boxes, they feature original labels that can be seen underneath the decoration. The figures and shapes were drawn first on paper with ink and watercolors, then cut out and applied to the boxes. Whatever the inspiration, these boxes from the collection of Hirschl & Adler Folk celebrate unfettered imagination and are much appreciated today.*

together in layers, then cut with a jigsaw and notch-carved to form the distinguishing diamond shapes.

Cherished then as now, yet used to their fullest, many personalized boxes have, thankfully, survived intact. Frequently, because they lack the sophistication and attention-getting embellishments of their more urbane counterparts, these humble folk pieces are overlooked. A closer scrutiny on the part of a perceptive buyer, however, can reveal thoroughly endearing expression and forms. Small inscriptions, painted scenes and symbols, unusual shapes, and miniature proportions all tell us of the joyous devotion lavished on these thoughtful pieces.

**Hudson River Valley Artistry**

*A verdant Hudson River Valley scene is painted on the sloping lid of this box, from the collection of Judith and James Milne, which was probably used as some sort of desk or office box in the 1930s and is still used for that purpose today. The lush scene contrasts with the simple construction and modest wood the box is made from—a case of folk art embellishing the most basic materials. Inside the box, a small shelf divides the interior space into two storage areas. This box was found at an estate sale in the Hudson River Valley, where it had fit into its natural surroundings for many years, reminding someone of the beauty just outside the door.*

## A Sailor's Fancy

*During long sea voyages, sailors would fill their spare hours doing fancy work with tools and materials readily available on board. Their practical skills of plaiting, knotting, and knitting quickly turned into art skills as they created decorative and useful gifts to take home to loved ones waiting ashore. These lovely boxes from the Forager House Collection are made from intricately knotted rope and incorporate sea-trade-related materials, such as the heart-shaped ivory pull.*

## Bounty of the Sea

*The dazzling bounty offered by the sea has long inspired sailors, professional artists, and amateur craftsmen alike to use shells for ornamentation. This early-twentieth-century shell box is a celebration of that tradition — gratifying the maker's fascination with nature and love of ornamentation, and serving as a proud souvenir of a trip to the beach. The generous size of this box from the collection of Ingrid Savage makes many uses possible, including storage for documents and letters, "toilette" articles, or a collection of whatnots.*

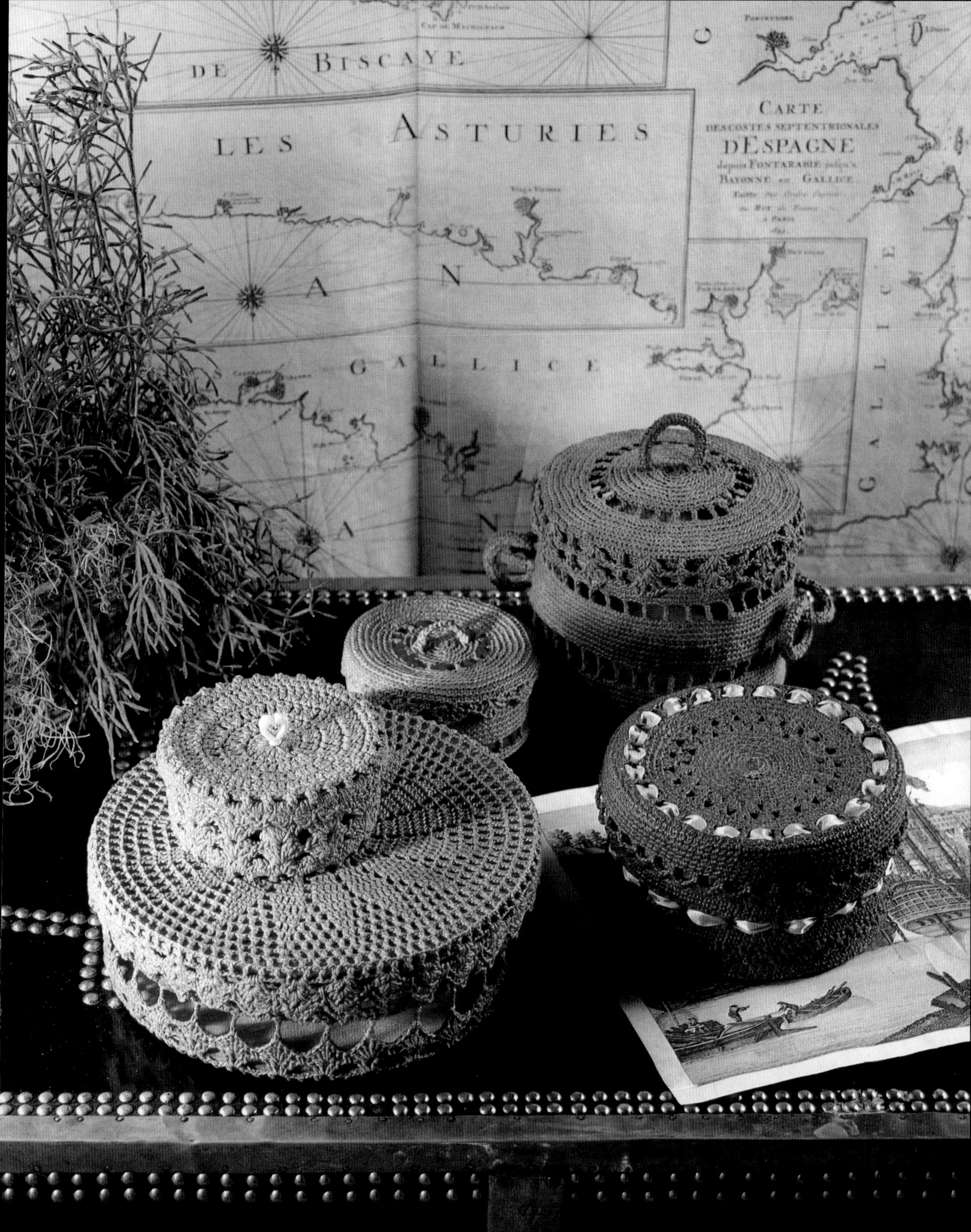
DE BISCAYE
LES ASTURIES
CARTE
D'ESPAGNE
GALLICE

**A Country Cousin**

*A clever and charming example of a "make-do," this handmade box from the collection of Judith and James Milne was fashioned from humble remnant materials and then adorned with carving, inlay, and painted decorations. The bottom of the box was made from the lid of a preexisting box; the formal effects created by the decoration give it a "country cousin" flavor. Adding to the box's charm is a line drawing of a church and steeple on the bottom, and an inscription inside the lid — "SUE" — with sums and figures written in pencil above the name. Did someone make this box as a gift for Sue? Or did she cleverly fashion it for her own purposes sometime in the early twentieth century? Box owners inevitably become imaginative detectives as they search for clues inside and out.*

**To Virtue and to Truth**

*This painted utility box from the collection of Hirschl & Adler Folk is attributed to Daniel Evans of Augusta, Maine. Miniature watercolor drawings of buildings have been mounted on the paperboard box. Each side is bordered by colored squares, and the rim of the box has a leaf-pattern border. Inscribed within a rectangle on the back panel are the words "Joseph Grant 1837." Inscribed on the underside of the lid is the following joyful discovery:*

Hail Penmanship,
thou lovely Art.

To please the eye,
instruct the heart.

Attention claim from
every Youth!!

Attach'd to Virtue
and to Truth.

To Mr. J. Grant
by W. D., Erfield

## The Little House

Great care was taken to construct and decorate this home-sweet-home, an American Indian house-shaped box with a hinged roof, made of birch bark, from the collection of Kelter-Malcé Antiques. Sweet grass bands the foundation, which was then sewn together with thread; dyed porcupine quills are applied to form flowers, windows, and a door. The quills appear in a series of short insertions, mimicking the outline and satin stitches used in embroidery. Dating from 1900, this truly charming piece of native work was done by North East Woodland Indians.

## Jigsaw Artistry

A cigar box, with some of its original markings still evident on the lid, forms the base of the pedestal box on the right, from the collection of Kelter-Malcé Antiques. From Pennsylvania circa 1920, the tramp art box has a lid that is composed of seven notch-carved layers and a six-layered knob. Constructed with glue and nails, this thoroughly original box has been stained to achieve its rich dark color. Also of the same period and location, and also from the collection of Kelter-Malcé Antiques, the tramp art wall box on the left features one long drawer spanning the length of the box with a second tier holding two smaller drawers that echo the popular medallion motif. Openings for candles on top of both drawer casings give the wall box a shrinelike appearance, perfect for a small portrait gallery.

## Symbolic Mysteries

*Initials, carved symbols, and painted adornments give rise to speculation about this pine fraternal wall box from the collection of Helaine and Burton Fendelman. Three connecting rings, containing the letters FLT, dominate the front of the open box. They are bordered by a book, a heart and hand, and a quill pen. Forming the one-piece open back is a cord, which rises from both sides to form an elaborate tassel in the center. Above the tassel is an eye, and, above it, stars and a moon. In the fleur-de-lis at the top is the aperture. Possibly an Odd Fellows box from New England that was made during the latter part of the nineteenth century, it may have adorned the home of an important member of a fraternal order, or possibly a lodge itself.*

## Stars and Stripes

*Resting between two mounted iron shooting-gallery targets, the applied notch-carved decoration of this small pine tramp art wall box, or "wall pocket," echoes the stark silhouette of the Indian's headdress, an artful grouping. Simple incised carvings on the back plate, which comes from the collection of Helaine and Burton Fendelman, include an American flag with seven stripes and twenty stars, as well as the initials J.F. One wonders what uses this box's maker had in mind.*

### Birthday Memories

*It appears that some thoughtful gift-giver fashioned this special box, part of my collection, using the artwork from floral greeting cards. On the inside of the lid, which is trimmed with foil and padded slightly, the front of a 1940s birthday card has been encased in Mylar and artfully blanket-stitched and crocheted together. The rest of the box is an unusual eight-sided bombé-shape construction. Colorful pansies are the primary floral motif, leaving one to wonder if the lucky recipient was especially fond of that flower.*

### Primitive Transformation

*The diminutive size, unpolished construction, and primitive painted decoration on this eighteenth-century wooden trinket box from the collection of Barbara Doherty bring to it a delightful combination of naiveté and elegance. Pleasing both in size and in shape, the box's slightly domed lid has primitive wire ring-hinges and a metal catch. The painted house and landscape design continues around all sides and onto the lid. Its place of honor on this antique shelf guarantees that it will not be overlooked or dwarfed by larger pieces.*

## Southern Victorian

*An unusual tiered table offers the perfect surface for displaying an equally unusual grouping of small Victorian treasures, a box collection from Kelter-Malcé Antiques among them. The three heart-shaped pasteboard boxes from the 1880s constitute a set, decorated with fabric appliqués over paper or other fabric. A box maker cut bright pieces of silk and satin into geometric shapes and industriously applied each shape to the boxes, bordering the designs with gold trim. The removable lids have die-cut scraps of paper on top and a lithograph or die-cut scrap pasted on the underside. The smallest box contains small dried leaves, presumably placed there by a long-ago owner somewhere in the South, possibly Tennessee. Two miniature book boxes covered in fancy brown velvet and decorated with German die-cut scraps of paper sit to the left of the large heart-shaped box.*

## Small Charm

*A pair of diminutive boxes is filled with detail. Both boxes feature a pasted-in illustration on their lids. The box on the left contains a tartan-design needle book that pulls out accordion-style. the box on the right contains a cloud of vibrant fuchsia lamb's wool, in which a tiny doll is nestled.*

**For Nostalgia's Sake**

*The 1939 World's Fair, held in New York's Flushing Meadow, has provided memorabilia collectors with some of the most graphically exciting souvenirs of the last two centuries. Two hatboxes from the collection of William H. Straus, offered as souvenirs to the throngs who came to the Fair seeking to find out about "the world of modernism," are displayed with a prizewinning poster. The guard's hat pictured is another example of the Fair's collectibles. An inviting aspect of twentieth-century memorabilia is the nostalgia it fosters for those who can look back and say, "I remember that . . ."*

# Homage to the Past:

*Newly Made American Boxes*

The many wonderful antique boxes that have survived over the decades—and even centuries—range from rare and coveted auction-house newsmakers to humbler objects that can still be found at flea markets and garage sales. Discovered and dusted off, these latter objects are loved for their charm and integrity, regardless of their cost or value. Unfortunately, the demand for antique boxes to display and use far exceeds the supply. Luckily, contemporary artisans and folk artists have been inspired by time-honored examples of the past to create replicas that show respect for the originals.

Many of today's artisans work with the same traditional methods and techniques that were employed many years ago. Box designs found in museum collections are faithfully reproduced, each step carried out by hand. Box makers comb antiques fairs and shops for vintage wallpapers and fabrics to cover their boxes. They seek out the most suitable woods and milk

**A Vintage Appeal**

*The sitting rooms and front parlors of houses in the second quarter of this century were warmed by curtains and slipcovers made from soft and elegant floral fabrics. Today, those same fabrics have found their way onto large hatboxes, giving them a nostalgic charm. Ivy Weitzman, and her company, A Touch of Ivy, was one of the first to scout out these lovely fabrics and to cover nesting boxes with them. As the supply of these fabrics grows scarce, boxes such as these from Sweet Nellie become all the more treasured.*

paints to create wooden boxes and small chests. Eschewing mass-produced imitations, they pay close attention to the detailing that distinguishes the originals, and they apply time-tested techniques of grain painting, inlay, and decorative design to embellish their work. Anyone who has ever made a Valentine by hand or embroidered the simplest design on the pocket of a child's overalls can appreciate the skill and devotion it required to produce handcrafts with integrity and taste.

This creative spirit is not limited to individuals and cottage industries in any particular area or geographic region. Newly made boxes are found from Maine to Montana. They may be made by fine artists, amateur carpenters, retired antiques dealers, hobbyists, architects, or former advertising executives! The box makers represented in this chapter may work alone and limit their production, or they may have a sophisticated assembly line behind them. The unifying factor is the boxes themselves—truly one-of-a-kind objects, painstakingly created by men and women who care about handcrafts and hope that their contribution will be cherished for many years to come.

An emerging number of today's box makers prefer to go beyond examples of the past to create boxes of their own unique invention. Inspired by their personal Muses, they may be influenced by past styles and designs; however, the boxes that result are original expressions for these artists. Experimental

**Neat and Tidy**

*Before the advent of spacious closets and chests of drawers, small pasteboard boxes held everything from lace collars to neatly pressed gloves. This glove box from Sweet Nellie, re-created by Berta Montgomery from old wallpaper (see caption, page 102), holds many of the same traditional accessories. A small box is still a neat and tidy way to deal with important possessions.*

**Romantic Visions**

*In the days of elegant hair combs and stiffly starched collars (like these collars from the collection of Ellen O'Neil), a box such as this one could have held either. This newly made comb/collar box from Sweet Nellie has been fashioned by Berta Montgomery after examples from the past and is covered in vintage wallpaper. Flat on one side and rounded on the other, the construction of such a box and the covering of it both inside and out require great dexterity and a large measure of patience.*

techniques in painting and woodworking are often combined with inspirations from textiles, the arts, and a multitude of cross-cultural influences. Many such box artists are shown with increasing regularity at galleries and museums across the country. Their innovative work is written about and given a recognition that box makers of yesteryear would envy, and the fascinating stories behind the boxes add immeasurably to our collective cultural heritage.

**Travel Mania**

*A sturdy bowler box of fifty years ago might have traveled far and wide, and would have the travel stickers to prove it. In a whimsical copy of an old men's hatbox, Paul's Hat Works, a men's hat shop in San Francisco, offers a reproduction complete with stickers that would impress the most worldly man.*

**A Re-creation**

*The delicate condition and rarity of original nineteenth-century bandboxes, not to mention their present-day prices, make the re-creation of those lovely storage and traveling boxes, like these examples from Sweet Nellie, all the more welcome. Berta Montgomery of Ohio, an antiques dealer for many years, eventually decided to manufacture her own. Having gathered together an enviable collection of vintage wallpaper, she started a business that would soon grow to include her husband and their daughters. Although many have tried to imitate Berta Montgomery's technique for making her boxes look timeworn, none has succeeded. Each of her boxes is signed and dated to avoid possible confusion with their original inspirations. The antique leather suitcases are from the collection of David Drummond.*

## Shaker Simplicity

*Pantry boxes made by the Shaker community were noted for their clean, simple design and their warm, rich colors, which have been copied by many artisans outside that small and close-knit group. When the Corcoran Gallery of Art in Washington, D.C., mounted a major exhibition devoted to Shaker design, a cottage industry from Maryland called The Friends was commissioned by the museum to create a large number of these handcrafted boxes to be sold in the gift shop.*

## A Respect for the Past

*The fine construction of Shaker boxes and a primitive painting style reminiscent of Rufus Porter come together in this contemporary maple and pine box from Sweet Nellie created by Irene Kiraloff and Karen Lindquist—otherwise known as The Friends. The artful grain painting on the lid of the box adds the finishing touch and makes the box suitable for any room and many functions. The box is shown next to two topiaries from Lexington Gardens and resting on an antique Shaker shag rug from Jones Road Antiques.*

### Victorian Memorabilia

*Antique and contemporary Victorian die-cut scraps have been artfully applied to a hardwood box using a traditional découpage technique by artisan Jeanette Sullivan, who calls her handcrafts business Southern Charm. The box, reminiscent of parlor boxes that were all the rage during the Victorian era, is finished with brass corner pieces and a brass clasp, then lined with vintage provincial fabric. It is from the collection of Hat & The Heart.*

### A Symbolic Suggestion

*The unmistakable language of the heart shape makes its meaning clear in this stack of paper-covered boxes from Sweet Nellie, a perfect gift. Susan Miller of Vermont, who works with her husband, Sven, to create boxes for their business, Open Cupboard, cuts and pastes cardboard into various shapes, then covers the resulting boxes in antique and reproduction wallpapers. The heart shape is, not surprisingly, her most popular one.*

### Trinkets and Charms

*Called "minikins" in colonial times, diminutive boxes like these from Sweet Nellie were handy for everything from hairpins to jewelry and small tokens. They could be stacked or packed for travel. Hundreds of these replica minikins are made each year by Open Cupboard, using their ample supply of dainty provincial wallcoverings to enhance the boxes' pretty appearance.*

### A Mantel Piece

*Whispers of another era, decorative boxes such as this one from Sweet Nellie are the perfect accessory and art object for today's living areas, gracing our mantels, chests, and tables and adding unique color and design elements to the overall scheme.*

## Wit and Whimsy

*The simple box form may be taken to delightful and fanciful extremes by imaginative invention. Heather Ramsey of Parvenue has created a group of truly original boxes with ornamentation that hints broadly of their contents. Displaying a variety of woods, wood veneers, and staining techniques, the resulting boxes, bought at the Store Next Door, are both art and useful objects. Clockwise from the top left: A box resembling a sturdy dock that could weather any hurricane is adorned with brass hardware accents in a suitable motif; there is little doubt about the use of this rectangular box, with its pencil-post legs; a charm box, with its glass-covered lid compartment revealing childhood treasures, has room for more treasures beneath the lid; and no stamps can get misplaced with this delightful and obvious reminder in box form.*

## Loving Commissions

For centuries, people have commissioned painters to immortalize their pets on canvas. Now, Sally Davis captures the likeness of household pets on small trinket boxes made of wood, artfully painted. Each box is given numerous coats of paint and sealer to achieve the vivid high-gloss finish. These boxes from Sweet Nellie are shown on top of a woven tapestry rug by Sara Hotchkiss.

## Age-Old Advancement

Inspired by a creature whose boxlike appearance calls out for a whimsical interpretation, wood-worker John Nelson constructs and paints his original "turtles" to resemble the real thing. A secret hiding place is revealed by pulling out the turtle's long neck. The rabbit pull-toy was made by the Sennebec Work-shop. The turtle boxes are from the Museum of American Folk Art Museum Shops.

### Artistic Endeavor

*Many of today's artists turn to the box form for artistic expression free of any functional value. Gardner Raphael III created this whimsical Wise Men box that bears a small banner inscribed* GOLD, FRANKINCENSE & MYRRH. *A window frame and the stars adorning the lid open the door to a fantasy for those dreaming of other gifts. The owner of this contemporary box, Linda Cheverton, was drawn to it at a benefit sale and was the lucky buyer.*

### Four-Sided Landscapes

*The passing of years very often imparts a gentle weathering to the finishes of old boxes. Contemporary folk painter Charles Muise, Jr., has admired and studied this natural aging process in many centuries-old pieces and has come up with his own technique for replicating it. By painting and then rubbing his surfaces to soften the images, Muise gives us memories from the past at affordable prices. The pine secretary in the background was also painted by Muise, whose pieces are signed and dated to avoid any confusion with the antiques that inspired them. The vase was made by contemporary potter Liz Lawrence.*

**Party Favors**

*This spirited and joyful grouping of acrylic-painted boxes from Sweet Nellie seems especially well suited to a festive occasion. Husband-and-wife team David Colombo and Carin Musacchia, fine artists from Boston, create their box forms from a clay-based paperboard. The designs are inspired by the many summers Carin has spent at her family's island cabin in Sweden, the land of painted furniture. Together, she and David hand-paint the designs on the boxes, which then become their bright and expressive canvases.*

**Black Magic**

*The owner of this contemporary box, Linda Cheverton, a collector of boxes old and new, found this exotic Voodoo box by multimedia artist Chuck Crosby while on vacation in New Orleans during Mardi Gras. The black figures are made of cut paper. They provide a striking contrast to the brightly colored painted patterns covering the surface of the box. The plastic Mardi Gras beads were thrown from floats to the crowd during the parade—a lucky catch!*

**Truly *Trompe l'oeil***

*Gleaming like true marble, Deborah Grenier's birch plywood faux marbre boxes truly fool the eye and deceive the touch. The artisan's intricate process, seen here on the tops of nine handsome square trinket boxes from Sweet Nellie, involves five coats of oil paint, seven layers of glazes, then skillful manipulation of the colors with feathers, sponges, and tissue paper. Then there are twelve sandings, one pumice rubbing, and, finally, a wax-polishing for the final, perfect finish. One understands how such a technique might become a lost art were it not for today's devotees.*

**Architectural Influences**

*Architect and furniture maker Daniel Hale shows the influence of the geometry he studied as part of his architectural training in the boxes he creates in limited editions. Although Hale is more widely recognized for his mastery of American folk-art forms, it is easy to recognize both Oriental and ancient motifs in his work as well. He uses bold layers of surface paint, often scratched through to layers below with combs, nails, and available workshop tools. His pieces — like these three boxes from Sweet Nellie — are distinguished by their fanciful geometric designs, black trim, and the small faces carved in relief. Many artists working today, Hale among them, prefer to limit the production of signed works, refusing to go beyond a set number no matter how strong the market is for any given piece.*

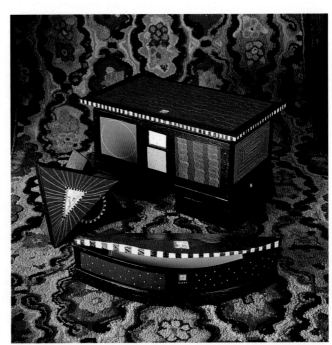

# Sources and
# Bibliography

# Sources for Boxes

**Cynthia Beneduce Antiques**
388 Bleecker Street
New York, NY 10014
(212) 645-5037

**Victoria Dinardo Fine Millinery**
68 Thompson Street
New York, NY 10012
(212) 334-9615

Barbara Doherty—Antiques
Tory Chimneys
Pearl Street, Box 974
Kennebunkport, ME 04046
(207) 967-4673
*By Appointment*

**E. G. H. Peter, Inc.**
Route 7
Sheffield, MA 01257
(413) 229-8881
*Open Thursday through Monday*

**Laura Fisher Antique Quilts
and Americana**
1050 Second Avenue, Gallery #57
New York, NY 10022
(212) 838-2596

**Forager House Collection**
P.O. Box 82
Washington Crossing, PA 18977
(215) 493-3007

**Hat & the Heart**
2806 East Madison
Seattle, WA 98112
(206) 325-9909

**Hirschl & Adler Folk**
851 Madison Avenue
New York, NY 10021
(212) 988-FOLK

**Jones Road Antiques**
1050 Second Avenue
New York, NY 10022
(212) 593-2246

**Kelter-Malcé**
361 Bleecker Street
New York, NY 10014
(212) 989-6760

**Judith and James Milne, Inc.**
506 East 74th Street
New York, NY 10021
(212) 472-0107

**Pantry & Hearth**
121 East 35th Street
New York, NY 10016
(212) 532-0535
*By Appointment*

**Susan Parrish Antiques**
390 Bleecker Street
New York, NY 10014
(212) 645-5020

**Store Next Door**
943 Madison Avenue
New York, NY 10021
(212) 606-0200

**Sweet Nellie**
1262 Madison Avenue
New York, NY 10128
(212) 876-5775

**William H. Straus**
1435 Lexington Avenue
New York, NY 10028
(212) 410-5682
*By appointment*

**James and Bonnie Udell**
(212) 840-1140
*By appointment*

# Books of Interest

Bedford, John.
**All Kinds of Small Boxes.**
New York: Walker and Co., 1964.

Bishop, Robert, and Patricia Coblentz.
**American Decorative Arts:
360 Years of Creative Design.**
New York: Harry N. Abrams, 1982.

Bishop, Robert,
and Judith Reiter Weissman.
**Folk Art.
The Knopf Collectors' Guides
to American Antiques.**
New York: Alfred A. Knopf, 1983.

Bowles, Ella Shannon.
**Homespun Handicrafts.**
Philadelphia and London:
J. B. Lippincott Co., 1931.

Carlisle, Lilian Baker.
**Hat Boxes and Bandboxes
at the Shelburne Museum.**
Shelburne Vt.: Shelburne Museum,
1960.

Christensen, Erwin O.
**The Index of American Design.**
New York: Macmillan, 1960.

Churchill, Edwin A.
**Simple Forms and Vivid Colors:
Maine Painted Furniture, 1800–1850.**
Augusta, Me.: The Maine State
Museum, 1983.

Cole, Brian.
**Boxes.**
Radnor, Pa.: Chilton Book Co., 1976.

**Collectors' Items from the
Saturday Book.**
New York: Macmillan, 1955.

Davis, Alec.
**Package and Print: The Development
of Container and Label Design.**
New York: Clarkson N. Potter, 1967.

D'Imperio, Dan.
**Country Antiques Companion.**
New York: Dodd, Mead, 1977.

Earle, Alice Morse.
**Home Life in Colonial Days.**
New York: Grosset & Dunlap, 1898.
Reprint. Stockbridge, Mass.: Berkshire
Traveller Press, 1944.

Earle, Alice Morse.
**Stage Coach and Tavern Days.**
New York: Macmillan, 1900.
Reprint. Detroit, Mich.: Singing Tree
Press, 1968.

Emmerling, Mary Ellisor.
**American Country: A Style and
Source Book.**
New York: Clarkson N. Potter, 1980.

**The Encyclopedia of Collectibles.**
Alexandria, Va.: Time-Life Books,
1978.

Evans, Paul.
**Art Pottery of the U.S.**
New York: Feingold & Lewis
Publishing Corp., 1987.

Fales, Dean A., Jr.
**American Painted Furniture,
1600–1880.**
New York: E. P. Dutton, 1972.

Fendelman, Helaine W.
**Tramp Art: An Itinerant's Folk Art.**
New York: E. P. Dutton, 1975.

Frere-Cook, Gerris, ed.
**The Decorative Arts of the Mariner.**
London: Cassell, 1966.

Gould, Mary Earle.
**Early American Wooden Ware and Other Kitchen Utensils.**
Springfield, Mass.: Pond-Ekberg Co., 1942.
Reprint. Rutland, Vt.: Charles E. Tuttle, 1962.

Greysmith, Barbara.
**Wallpaper.**
New York: Macmillan, 1976.

Harbeson, Georgiana Brown.
**American Needlework.**
New York: Bonanza Books, 1938.

Henderson, Marjorie, and Elizabeth Wilkinson.
**Whatnot: A Compendium of Victorian Crafts and Other Matters.**
New York: William Morrow, 1977.

Hornung, Clarence.
**Treasury of American Design.**
2 vols.
New York: Harry N. Abrams, 1972.

Houart, Victor.
**Sewing Accessories: An Illustrated History.**
London: Souvenir Press, 1984.

Kassay, John.
**The Book of Shaker Furniture.**
Amherst, Mass.: University of Amherst Press, 1980.

Ketchum, William C., Jr.
**American Basketry and Woodenware.**
New York: Macmillan, 1974.

Ketchum, William C., Jr.
**Boxes.**
The Smithsonian Illustrated Library of Antiques.
New York: Cooper-Hewitt Museum, 1982.

Ketchum, William C., Jr.
**The Catalog of American Antiques.**
New York: Rutledge Books, distributed by Scribner, 1977.

Klamkin, Marian.
**The Collector's Book of Boxes.**
New York: Dodd, Mead, 1970.

Klamkin, Marian.
**Shaker Folk Art & Industries.**
New York: Dodd, Mead, 1972.

Kovel, Ralph, and Terry Kovel.
**American Country Furniture, 1780–1875.**
New York: Crown Publishers, 1965.

Kovel, Ralph, and Terry Kovel.
**Kovel's Know Your Antiques.**
Rev. ed. New York: Crown Publishers, 1981. (Previously published as **Know Your Antiques**, 1967.)

Lichten, Frances.
**Decorative Arts of Victoria's Era.**
New York and London: Charles Scribner's Sons, 1950.

Lichten, Frances.
**Folk Art of Rural Pennsylvania.**
New York: Charles Scribner's Sons, 1946.

Lipman, Jean, and Alice Winchester.
**The Flowering of American Folk Art, 1776~1876.**
New York: Viking Press, A Studio Book, 1974.

Little, Nina Fletcher.
**Neat and Tidy: Boxes and Their Contents in Early American Homes.**
New York: E. P. Dutton, 1980.

McClellan, Elizabeth.
**Historic Dress in America, 1607–1870.**
New York and London: Benjamin Blom, 1904~1910.

McClinton, Katharine Morrison.
**Antique Collecting for Everyone.**
New York: McGraw-Hill, 1951.

McClinton, Katharine Morrison.
**Antiques Past and Present.**
New York: Clarkson N. Potter, 1971.

McClinton, Katharine Morrison.
**Collecting American Victorian Antiques.**
New York: Charles Scribner's Sons, 1966.

Morton, Barbara M.
**Down East Netting.**
Camden, Me.: Down East Books, 1988.

Nutting, Wallace.
**Furniture of the Pilgrim Century.**
Framingham, Mass.: Old America Company, 1924.

Peter, Mary.
**Collecting Victoriana.**
New York: Frederick A. Praeger, 1968.

Phipps, Frances.
**Colonial Kitchens, Their Furnishings, and Their Gardens.**
New York: Hawthorn Books, 1972.

**A Place for Everything: Chests and Boxes in Early Colonial America.**
Winterthur, Del.: The Henry Francis du Pont Winterthur Museum, 1986.

Randier, Jean.
**Nautical Antiques for the Collector.**
Garden City, N.Y.: Doubleday, 1977.

Ross, Pat.
**Hannah's Fancy Notions**
(for children ages 8–11).
New York: Viking Penguin, 1988.

Schaffner, Cynthia V. A., and Susan Klein.
**Folk Hearts.**
New York: Alfred A. Knopf, 1984.

Vincent, Margaret.
**The Ladies' Work Table.**
Allentown, Pa.: Allentown Art Museum, 1988.

Waring, Janet.
**Early American Stencils on Walls and Furniture.**
New York: Dover Publications, 1968.

Warnick, Kathleen, and Shirley Nilsson.
**Legacy of Lace.**
New York: Crown Publishers, 1988.

Whiting, Gertrude.
**Old Time Tools and Toys of Needlework.**
New York: Dover Publications, 1971.

# Articles Worth Mentioning

Brown, Donna Keith.
**"Decorated Tinware."**
*Old Sturbridge Visitor* 26, no. 1.

Coffin, Margaret Mattison.
**"Decorated Tinware."**
*Antiques*, August 1953.

Deitz, Paula.
**"Decorative Boxes House
Secrets and Surprises."**
*New York Times*, August 27, 1989.

Fitch, Josephine Hoyt.
**"Some Old Paper Boxes."**
*Antiques*, August 1928.

Flohr, Lewis B.
**"Shipping Eggs by Parcel Post."**
U.S. Dept. of Agriculture. Farmer's
Bulletin 594, June 4, 1914.

Frary, I. T.
**"Stagecoach Luggage."**
*Antiques*, August 1940.

Frazer, Esther Stevens.
**"The Golden Age of Stencilling."**
*Antiques*, April 1922.

Johnson, Bruce E.
**"Pottery with a Purpose."**
*Country Living*, January 1989.

Miniter, Edith.
**"When Women's Work
Was Never Done."**
*Antiques*, September 1926.

**"Porcupine Quills Query."**
*Antiques*, April 1939.

Roe, F. Gordon.
**"In the Likeness of Books."**
*Antiques*, February 1940.

Schaffner, Cynthia.
**"At Home with Antiques."**
*House Beautiful*, January 1987.

Snow, Julia D. Sophronia.
**"The Clayton's Ascent
Bandbox."**
*Antiques*, September 1928.

Swan, Mabel M.
**"The Village Tinsmith."**
*Antiques*, March 1928.